Blueprint for Success in Business

E. P. Whitney

UNIVERSITY PRESS OF AMERICA,® INC.
Lanham • Boulder • New York • Toronto • Plymouth, UK

Copyright © 2010 by
University Press of America,® Inc.
4501 Forbes Boulevard
Suite 200
Lanham, Maryland 20706
UPA Acquisitions Department (301) 459-3366

Estover Road
Plymouth PL6 7PY
United Kingdom

British Library Cataloging in Publication
Information Available

Library of Congress Control Number: 2009931482
ISBN: 978-0-7618-4746-5 (paperback : alk. paper)
eISBN: 978-0-7618-4747-2

Contents

iii

Foreword: The Blueprint for Financial Management

It is estimated that seventy-five percent of the businesses that go bankrupt do so because they have not properly planned and prepared an adequate budget. Ninety percent of the remaining twenty five percent go bankrupt because they failed to monitor and adjust their budgets adequately.

The budget is the blue print for success in business. In Western Society, everything is business; and to be successful in any enterprise whether it is a corporation, small business, nonprofit institution or one's personal affairs, it is necessary to plan and employ sound business principles. This unit presents the fundamental business principles and practices necessary to plan and develop a budget to guide the successful operation of a business enterprise.

Finally, as concerns preparation of this text, I would like to express gratitude to my editor, Deborah S. Nash, for her valuable assistance in helping finalize it and move it forward.

Chapter One

The Budget

Financial Management starts with a budget! The budget is the "blueprint" for the operation of any business or organization. It is the plan for conducting the affairs of the business. The "budget process" is perhaps even more important than the budget itself.

STRATEGIC PLANS

The budget process starts with the strategic long-term objectives and purposes of the business or organization. The strategic plan is the key to all business activity. It should be carefully developed and clearly expressed.

The strategic plan defines the purpose of the business or organization; that is to say, its *reason for existence*. The business enterprise should meet a need. This need should be the main reason for establishing the enterprise. The desire to make a profit is an assumed reason for existence and need not be stated. However, strategies relating to how your enterprise can be most efficient, and how it can meet the need better than the competition should be included.

Once developed, the strategic plan should be prominently displayed at all decision-making functions and should be considered when making any and all operational decisions. Failure to follow this simple, basic principle leads to abuses and counter-productive activity.

Example #1: Strategic Plan for the Real Estate Agency

The purpose of the Acme Real Estate Agency is to sell single family dwellings to financially qualified buyers in the county of Madison, New York.

The agency will serve any person requesting their services that have been financially qualified by a Madison County Bank. Office hours will be from 9 a.m. to 7 p.m. Monday through Friday, and 8 a.m. to 12 noon on Saturday. Agents will be available for appointments any time at the convenience of the client Monday through Saturday.

All Agents representing Acme must have a valid New York State Real Estate Salesman License.

Example #2: Strategic Plan for the ABC Day Care Center

The purpose of the ABC Day Care Center is to provide a secure environment for the children of working mothers in the Thomas Jefferson Housing Development in Big Town, USA without discrimination.

The Center will operate 5 days a week (Monday through Friday) from 7:30 a.m. to 5:30 p.m.

Enrollment will be limited to children between 2 and 4 years of age.

OPERATIONAL PLANS

Once the strategic plan is established, an operational plan should be developed. Operational plans are usually developed for specific periods of time. The Long-Term Operational Plan is generally developed for a 5 or 10 year period of time, the current operational plan for only a one-year period.

Long-term operational plans generally relate to capital considerations regarding growth and expansion. Short-term operational plans relate to day-to-day activities and maintenance of the business or institution.

The basic rule for the long-term operational plan is that it be in complete harmony with the strategic plan. Unlike the strategic plan, the long-term operational plan is less idealistic; it deals with targets and goals rather than philosophical objectives.

Long-term predictions are not completely reliable and the long-term operational plan will usually have to be monitored and adjusted on a yearly basis to keep it realistic. Many institutions have suffered serious losses as a result of failure to re-evaluate goals and postpone them and adjust to changing conditions.

Capital considerations involve the purchase or lease of buildings and equipment. The amount of "space," the accommodations of that space, and the equipment necessary to fulfill the objectives of the strategic plan must be determined and provided for before operations can begin.

Additional considerations such as a "feasibility study," surveys, etc. aimed at determining the needs and requirements for successfully operating the business or organization should also be addressed.

A feasibility study can be as simple as a brain storming session which explores the pros and cons of the planned operation. A survey can be as simple as a polling a sample of the population that you plan to serve regarding any questions that might have an impact on the successful operation of your enterprise. Basic questions to be asked might include, for example, "Do you ever need the service or product that you plan to provide?" "How often do you secure the service or product that you plan to provide?" and "Where do you currently secure the service or product that, you plan to provide?" Information is intelligence, and the more information of this nature that you can gather, the more intelligent your plans will be.

The general needs and expansion plans would no doubt be well discussed and evident before even the strategic plan is completed. The task at hand would then be to put these needs and plans into detailed, written form. This serves as a starting point for operation of the business or organization.

In the case of an already-established institution, strategic and long term operational plans have most likely already been made and an operational budget prepared. It is then a simple matter to review them together with previous annual budgets in preparation for developing a new budget.

Example #3: Long-Term Operational Plan for the Acme Real Estate Agency

The Agency will rent 1000 square feet of office space at 213 Broadway for $1,000 a month.

The agency will start with 2 telephone lines, one office manager and 3 sales agents. The manager will be paid $400 a week plus 1% of gross sales. Sales Representatives will work on a commission basis of 6% of individual gross sales.

The Agency will charge clients a commission of 10% of gross selling price. Listings will be restricted to single-family dwellings within the boundaries of Madison County.

Example #4: Long-Term Operational Plan
for the ABC Day Care Center

Lease two rooms in the Thomas Jefferson Community Building for three years at $100 a month.

Enrollment limited to a total of 30 children.

Three competent day care providers will be hired at $100 per week.

Contract with neighborhood elementary school cafeteria to provide lunches for the children ages 2 through 4 at $1.00 per meal.

Levy a charge of $20 per child per week.

Chapter Two

The Annual Budget

The short-term operational plan is more generally known as the annual budget. This budget is the "blue print" or operating plan for the management team for the next fiscal period.

The annual budget process starts at the grass roots level, at the lowest rung on the management chain. Not only do these front-line troops give a valuable perspective, but involving this population in the budgeting process helps to develop the teamwork and cooperation necessary to successfully conduct operations.

Each grass roots employee should develop goals and objectives for their individual job along with a detailed estimate of the funds needed to achieve each primary and secondary objective. For maximally effective planning, the budgets should be developed on a monthly basis and monthly data should then be added in to then determine the annual budget. Monthly figures are of great help to upper management in developing cash-flow estimates, as well as in the budget monitoring.

The practice of involving everyone in the enterprise in the budgeting (planning) process is a revolutionary concept, one that is often opposed by old line management; still, it has many advantages.

First, it makes it clear that each employee is a part of the enterprise and has an informed interest in its success. Second, it makes it easier for management to validly assess the competence and suitability of a given employee for the position he or she is to fill. Lastly, it makes available vital information that management was perhaps not previously aware of.

INDIVIDUAL BUDGET ESTIMATES

Example #5: The Individual Budget Estimate

Employee:

Job Description

Resources Needed to Perform Your Tasks

Est. Cost:

Est. Cost:

Note: Employees in a small business enterprise play a much bigger role in the success of the enterprise than do the employees of a large corporation! They are generally expected to perform a wider range of services, are often a vital part of the public image of the enterprise, and their loyalty and good will has a big impact on the successful operation of the enterprise. Whatever can be done to increase the employee's positive contribution to the enterprise will result in an increase in the probability of success of the enterprise.

TO THE FINANCIAL MANAGER

The budget is normally prepared for a one year period. But a breakdown into monthly budgets can be enormously helpful in monitoring the budget especially in the progressive state of the ESP Approach to budgeting presented later. Corresponding monthly cash flow budgets will also be most helpful to the financial manager.

Chapter Three

Review of Previous Years' Activities

The review of previous years' activities can reveal income and expense patterns that will be most helpful in estimating and forecasting. It has been wisely stated that 'the future is merely a continuation of the past.' Past experience should be the starting point for every annual budget. Also, where a business is starting up, data on the past experience of similar businesses can be most helpful.

The budget itself is merely a statement containing all of the probable sources of income for the year with anticipated amounts for each; and an estimate of all of the expenses that would be incurred during the year. As a first step, previous budget and financial statements should be reviewed and analyzed. Reasons for variance on each and every budget item should be determined, and consideration should be given to any action that might be taken to improve the situation. This review of past experience can be one of the most important activities in the budget process.

Past experience is then tempered with relevant factors that are currently affecting similar institutions and could affect future operations. These could include existing economic conditions and overall predictions for the future. Also included might be any major shifts or developments, either current or anticipated such as the influence or potentially adverse impact of a competitor.

Comments from employees at the grass roots level should be taken very seriously. Individual problems and contingencies should be thoroughly discussed and possible solutions presented.

Another consideration to be addressed would be the activities that you have planned that will affect your own operations (i.e., those that could enhance support for your business or organization such as sales campaigns, etc.) Consideration should also be given to coordination of activities on the community, state and national levels.

Forecasting is a most unreliable practice. Even the diluting of an estimate into a "range" must be recognized as a matter of probability, not a certainty

Chapter Four

An ESP Approach
to Budgeting

One approach to budgeting that is extremely helpful in the vital budget-monitoring function is called the ESP Approach to Budgeting. While the name rightly alludes to the non-absolute aspect of budgeting, it is perhaps one of the most realistic ways of addressing the 'budget problem.'

E stands for Existence, S, for Survival, and P, for Progressive. On this approach, three separate budgets are prepared.

The first budget, that of *Existence*, is based upon the bare objective of holding on until better times come along. It requires that a maximally conservative estimate of income be made; only expenses that must absolutely be paid are to be included. Even the depreciation allowance for equipment, buildings, etc. is eliminated. The luxury of insurance, unless mandated by law, is also not included. Under this budget, a business or institution would have limited life. Its only hope for continuance would be a drastic change for the better.

The second budget, that of *Survival,* includes a more optimistic estimate of income; but it is limited to only those expenses that would make it possible to maintain the status quo.   Consideration for the maintenance of equipment, buildings, etc. would be included as would reasonable insurance costs.

The third budget, the *Progressive* one, includes an optimistic estimate of income which would cover the "wish list" of projects and operations that the business or organization would like to engage in. After general operational costs are accounted for, desired projects are prioritized to assist with the budget-monitoring process.

Chapter Five

Analyzing the Budget Data

As previously noted, the budget itself is simply a statement of the anticipated Income, Costs and Expenses. It generally takes the form of the Company Profit and Loss Statement. (Also called the Income Statement or the Operational Income and Expense Statement.) When presented in this form, it is easier to monitor and compare the budget with Interim Profit and Loss Statements.

Anticipated Income is derived from the Forecasting Analysis and expenses are derived and summarized from Individual Budget Estimates.

FORECASTING

Forecasting is the scientific process of making intelligent guesses. No one can predict the future with complete certainty, but some guesses are definitely better than others. When careful analysis is made and all factors are considered, predictions can be made with reasonable accuracy.

If a locomotive was speeding down the tracks at 60 miles per hour and a car was stalled on the track 100 feet ahead, one could make a reasonably reliable prediction that it would strike the car. If the locomotive was traveling only at 30 miles per hour and the car was stalled 200 feet ahead, the prediction would be considerably less reliable. If several men were standing by ready to push the car off the track, it would be even less reliable. The longer the time and the greater the number of contingent factors involved, the less reliable the prediction will be.

TREND ANALYSIS

One basic technique for forecasting future business operations is Trend Analysis. In its simplest terms, it is the plotting of an activity (such as sales) over a period of time to determine a pattern, then extrapolating that pattern into the future. If, for example, the Radio Corporation has increased its income by 10% each year for the past five years and last year's income was 10.8 million, then a simple projection of another 10% increase for next year for a forecast of next year's income at 11.88M (determined by adding 10.8 plus 10% of 10.8 or 1.08) would be an example of an application of trend analysis for forecasting.

If additional information were available, such as an expected division in the corporation whereby radio stations generating 20% of the corporation's income would be dropped from their network, it would be reasonable to revise this simple projection downward to 9.504M (determined by subtracting 20% of 11.88 or 2.376 from 11.88)

If then, the corporation planned to counter with an advertising campaign expected to recover half of the anticipated loss, it would be reasonable to adjust the forecast upward 10% to 10.45M (determined by adding 10% of .9504 to 9,504 and rounding off)

If one were forecasting the income of a church, a Trend Analysis would be most appropriate for Pledge income, plate collections and fund raisers as well as for any investment income that the church would expect. This figure would be adjusted to reflect the increase or decrease in membership, the deletion or addition of fund raising projects, or any other factors that would affect the forecast. Brainstorming to determine factors that would increase or decrease any item should be undertaken with great care if it is to produce realistic results. For example, a nearby church might be adding or expanding a similar fund raising project, but that project may or may not have an impact on its anticipated income from fundraising. Considerations must be based on as much factual information as can be obtained.

Chances are very slim that a financial manager can ever be completely accurate with any forecast for the future; still, this is no reason to neglect the forecasting function. It is important to have plans and goals even if we feel certain that they will change.

The forecast at least gives a mark at which to aim, a point around which one can adjust one's efforts. Forecasting generally refers to predicting income and estimating, to anticipating expenses. The fundamentals of predicting the future are, however, basically the same whether once is concerned with income or expenses. Predicting expenses can be somewhat more accurate as management generally has greater control over them than it has over income.

SEGMENT AND CATEGORICAL COST ANALYSIS

The forecasting function often involves extended analysis and requires managerial decisions in order to make adjustments and changes to operational plans. Two types of analysis that are often used by the financial manager when planning and forecasting are Segment Analysis and Categorical Cost Analysis.

Segment Analysis

Segment Analysis simply refers to a breakdown of operations into independent units or segments. In a county government, for example, the most common breakdown is by departments. (i.e., Public Works, Water, Administration, etc.) In a school, it is usually by function. (i.e. faculty, administration, maintenance, etc.) In a small business enterprise, it would most likely parallel individual expense items.

If the enterprise had two or more distinct operational functions (such as purchasing and sales, or wholesale and retail) it would be wise to break down the expenses into separate operational functions. This would give additional data to analyze operations and so improve efficiency. Allocating expenses to each operation helps to increase the accuracy of future forecasts as well as to isolate possible trouble spots.

Categorical Cost Analysis

Categorical Cost Analysis refers to the analysis of individual expenses. Consider the following example: Records reveal that gasoline expenses for the ABC Trucking Company have increased 8% while maintenance expenses have increased by 40%. Further analysis reveals that the item causing the increase in maintenance was engine repair. Trucks were in fact being retained beyond the normal replacement period and consequently repair costs were far above normal. A decision must be made as to whether or not to replace the trucks. This is a factor which, when included in a forecast of expenses, will result in greater accuracy and also provide a guideline for more efficient management of operations.

An analysis of individual expenses helps to pinpoint inefficiencies and determine responsibilities which can effect more efficient management as well as produce more accurate forecasts.

As previously cited, the forecast is the goal. The more the goal is analyzed, the more accurate the forecast can be and consequently the more efficient the operation of the business or organization can be.

Chapter Six

Analysis of Past Operations

An extremely important part of the budget process is the review and analysis of data from previous years' operations.

This review should start with a comparison of each of the new budget items over against previous years' budgets. Were any items that were contained in previous years' budgets left out of this year's budget? If so, why? And, is there good reason not to include them in the current budget? Also, are there any items on the current budget that were not included in previous years'? If so, why? Perhaps there is good reason to include them in this year's budget.

Further analysis should be made of all variances, both positive and negative.

An operating expense, for example, may be under budget and appear to be a favorable variance. Complete investigation may, however, reveal that a necessary operation was not completely fulfilled and that the net result on that operation could be negative and so affect the company's financial picture overall.

Likewise, an income item may be over budget. This might be the result of a factor that should have been taken into consideration in forecasting; its inclusion in next year's budget could make for a more reliable prediction. It could also reveal that there had been some foul play in previous years.

In sum, complete analysis of all variances can be very useful to the financial manager and should never be ignored.

Chapter Seven

Monitoring the Budget

Real management skills come into play in budget monitoring where actual income and expenses are compared to budgeted income and expenses. Every variance must be analyzed and the reason for it determined. If possible, steps should be taken to bring variances into line. In some cases, adjustments have to be made to guide operations for the remainder of the year.

Variance trends usually indicate a need for adjustment. A deficit in income calls for immediate action to either increase income or decrease expenses. A runaway expense item can indicate a serious operational problem for a particular unit, one that must be dealt with promptly.

Very seldom will actual income and expenses be in perfect agreement with the budget. This, however, is no reason not to investigate every variance even those which are desirable, (i.e., income over budget/expenses under budget) Even desirable variances can indicate problems. Expenses which prove to be under budget can indicate that a particular unit is not functioning properly. It may indeed be failing to perform a very necessary operation to the full extent necessary for successful total operation of the institution!

In every case, variances should be investigated, even items that are 'on the line.' Management is a dynamic function, and monitoring the budget is one of its most crucial activities. If prompt attention and consideration is given to any problem when it first emerges, the chances for an effective solution with minimal loss of operational efficiency are greater than they would otherwise be.

THE COVER-UP

One of the greatest temptations in financial management is to avoid exposing information that reflects unfavorably upon management and its practices. Very often, only top management is aware of the abuse and incompetence that can result in excessive costs or depletion of funds. There is sometimes even the temptation to cover up dishonesty, a practice which can provide an individual with personal gain and a false sense of security. Even the welfare of a friend or relative may be a motivation in this. Because this sort of risk is ever present, a system of internal controls should always be installed and observed.

INTERNAL CONTROL

Several basic rules should be followed in providing internal control within an institution:

1. Income and Expense functions should be kept separate. They are operations which are independent of each other. Anyone charged with responsibility for recording and receiving income should never be given the opportunity to exercise control or influence over outgoing payments, and vice-versa.
2. Wherever possible and practicable, a system of checks and balances should be installed respective to each function. For example, any checks which are paid out should require two (2) signatures; bills should be approved for payment by a unit manager responsible, then sent to the business office where the expense is checked against the budget.
3. The accounting function should be kept separate from the administrative function; these, too, are independent operations. The treasurer's office is responsible for keeping accurate records of income and expenses and for providing full disclosure in periodic reports. The treasurer

should not exercise any control over management and its activities!

Often a treasurer is one of the most competent financial managers in the institution and his advice may be crucial to its successful management. However, his or her role should be strictly advisory and he must not become a part of the management operation. Doing so could compromise his or her function as the guardian of the integrity of the financial records.

4. The process of developing the budget should be an independent function as well. To be sure, it requires input from management and operational units, but the process should in no way be controlled by either group. Personnel in charge of the budget process should carry out their duties objectively. The initial budget should be presented by the budget officer to the appropriate body for approval. All responsible parties should have the opportunity to be heard by the approving body before a decision is made on either adopting or rejecting it. Ideally, such a process should be conducted by an outside agency in much the same manner as an audit.

Once a budget is adopted, it is management's responsibility to operate as the budget mandates. If it has been properly prepared, the budget should indeed be considered a mandate rather than a target or only a vague goal.

Some changes in the budget are inevitable, variations will occur. However, management should be held accountable for any and all of them; and full explanations should be forthcoming from management to the budget-approving body for them. In the case of government, for example, if Congress approves the budget, the executive branch should be accountable to the Congress for any deviations from it. These should also be made public, together with appropriate explanations for them.

The larger the institution and the further its rank and file are removed from the budget process, the greater the opportunity for abuse and dishonesty. Effective and efficient management is difficult and costly, but failure to make the effort is far more so. The key to honest management of any institution is participation; and the key to effective participation is education.

RECORDING FINANCIAL INFORMATION

Proper recording of financial information is the backbone of the financial management system. In the absence of detailed information, management is left to rely merely on intuition in making vital decisions.

While it is not necessary for management to become proficient and understand all aspects of Double Entry Accrual Accounting, it should most definitely have a good understanding of its company's or institution's accounting system. Any manager who does not possess such knowledge should seek to develop expertise in this area before accepting any responsibility for the financial operations of an institution.

For anyone without formal accounting training, it is recommended that they secure a copy of the educational card game, "CEO."[1] It presents the basic accounting principles, exclusive of unnecessarily detailed functions such as debits and credits. It can be mastered through self-study and includes a set of self-tests for achievement.

The chart of accounts is key to understanding the accounting system for any particular institution. In addition to the general accounts as indicated in the above cited educational game, there should also be one titled Unbudgeted Expenditures. Any transaction that does not fit into the listed chart of accounts should be charged to this. Analysis of it can be of great value to management. It will pinpoint misappropriations, incompetency, and inadequate control as well as the astute managerial adjustments that have produced benefits and obviated against losses.

Furthermore, it is essential that charges be made to an appropriate account. Any question as to whether or not an expense should be charged to a budgeted account should be resolved by charging it to Unbudgeted Expenditures. Decisions as to which account will be charged are to be made by management in an open review of the budget report. Particular care should be taken to avoid any budget adjustments at the recording level. Management should have no part in the recording function. Any "juggling" of expenses by charging to a line item that is below budget amount or charging a budget line item for an unbudgeted expense constitutes the beginning of cover-up and leads to false reports and dishonesty. In other words, the recording function is the frontline defense against misappropriation and mismanagement of finances.

Most institutions of any size will have computerized accounting systems that can at least appear to take care of all of the necessary record keeping activity. While these systems do a great job of keeping records, they still are no substitute for a thorough understanding of the accounting system and the computer print-out. The print-out is only as good as the data which has been entered. It is part of management's responsibility to be on top of the recordkeeping function and to make adjustments and corrections as needed. In the absence of a thorough understanding of the accounting system, management is not able to verify any of the vital information regarding the financial activities of the institution.

BUDGET STABILIZATION STRATEGIES

Balancing the Budget can be one of life's most frustrating activities. Often, a corrective adjustment at mid-year aimed at insuring that operations will end the year in balance actually fails to achieve the desired results. As year-end nears, frantic and sometimes irrational actions are taken in the face of a larger and ever expanding deficit. The result can be even greater frustration when the same sequence of events repeats itself the next year.

A balanced budget is somewhat like a perpetual motion machine. Some attempts to achieve balance do come close, but no one ever seems to come up with the perfect solution. Perhaps such a solution will never be found. There are some measures however that can help to reduce large deficits. They are referred to as budget stabilization strategies.

Reserve for Economic Fluctuations

One simple strategy is to set up a 2–5% reserve for economic fluctuations. This is a line item "surplus" figure (2–5% of the total budget). If it is not used in one year, it is carried over and accumulated for subsequent years.

Budget Cushions

Another strategy is to use budget cushions:

1) Contingency items can be included. These are line items for possible expenses, those that might occur and over which one cannot reasonably be expected to have any control.
2) Discretionary items also need to be included in a budget, i.e. line items that would be used in the second half of the year if funds are available.

3) A 2% to 5% overage in line items can also be planned for those items that are most difficult to accurately forecast.

Using the ESP Approach

A most effective strategy is the ESP approach to budgeting noted previously.

All of these strategies require more income to be budgeted. The other strategic approach is to control expenditures. This is most difficult because it conflicts with our established mind set on personal gain, competition, and achievement.

Handling a Positive Balance

A major challenge in financial management is to establish the concept that a positive balance at the end of the year is not a tragedy. This can be accomplished by rewarding instead of punishing those responsible for the surplus.

In most budget systems, the manager who does not use up all of his allocations in one fiscal period will most likely have a smaller allocation the following period! This provides little motivation for frugal management. If, instead, management is guaranteed that this will not be the practice, and a manager is given a bonus, then a greater number of managers may end the year with positive balances. If one half of that bonus was designated for the manager to award to subordinates who assisted with this accomplishment, it might provide the impetus for the cooperation needed for such an achievement!

Opponents of such a plan maintain that awards and bonuses are given for action above and beyond the line of duty; and that it is the duty of every manager to be frugal and responsible. The reality here is that most managers believe there maximum duty is to stay within the budget.

The generally recognized key to budget control is effective budget monitoring. One of the keys to effective budget monitoring is frequent and accurate financial reports.

Key Item Sample Report

In massive line item budgets, frequent and accurate financial reports are very difficult and extremely costly to produce. A suggested technique to help resolve this problem is the KIS Variance Report. (Key Item Sample Report)

The KIS Variance Report should reflect the net variance of actual expenditures to date from the budget to date for selected, key budget items. This gives management a current view of budget performance in much the same way the Dow Jones average gives investors a current picture of the Stock Market performance. A large positive variance calls for an effort to examine over budget items and develop corrective strategies.

Selecting Key Budget Items

The KIS Variance Report System starts with the selection of key budget line items. These must be selected with care to give a representative sampling of the total budget. They are then monitored on a daily basis to determine the variance for each; the net total variance is then obtained by adding the positive variances and subtracting the negative ones. A simple computer program can be used to manage data: The budget-to-date amount can be entered at the beginning of the year with actual amounts then entered daily. This figure can provide a reasonably accurate assessment of budget performance, data that is readily available to management and all other concerned parties to expose the threat of deficits at the earliest point possible.

Absolute financial control is a goal that may never be reached. Still, every institution must constantly aim at it.

NOTE

1. "CEO," an educational card game by E.P. Whitney, available at college bookstores.

Discussion Questions

1. Should a non-profit institution have financial management as one of its major concerns?
2. Should the annual budget be a target or a mandate?
3. What are the key elements involved in the budgeting process?
4. How important is the strategic plan for a non-profit institution?
5. What is the ESP Approach to budgeting?
6. What is budget monitoring?
7. Is there a need for internal control in the financial management of a non-profit institution?
8. What are the steps in the budgeting process?

KEY TO DISCUSSION QUESTIONS

1. Efficient financial management is necessary for the effective operation of any institution in a free economic society. However, this function should always be kept subservient to the main purpose of the institution. (e.g. hospitals, schools, churches).
2. A budget should be considered a mandate in that management should do everything in its power to operate within it. However, circumstances may make it necessary for them to make some adjustments in order to achieve some vital objectives and/or avert disaster.
3. The most important element in the budgeting process is to involve the total institution in the planning process.
4. The strategic plan sets forth the purpose and objective of the institution. This is the it exists at all!
5. The ESP Approach to budgeting requires the preparation of 3 budgets; one to keep the institution in *existence* until times get better; the second to allow it to *survive*; and the third to allow it to *expand and progress*.
6. Budget monitoring is the process whereby management compares actual income and expenses during a given fiscal period against amounts budgeted for them.
7. Internal control is the preventive measure(s) taken to avoid abuse and dishonesty in the financial management of an institution.

8. Steps in the budget process:
   a) Grass roots-level management prepares monthly operational plans together with estimated cost for each activity.
      i) Upper management can make recommendations and mandate tasks and activities that should/must be accomplished.
      ii) Upper management may limit expenses of a unit.
   b) The budget is then passed up the management ladder and input is added at each level.
   c) The complete budget is compiled by budget committee or CEO.
   d) It is monitored during the year and
      i) Each variance is analyzed
      ii) Adjustments are made as appropriate
      iii) Overall review is conducted

Appendix: Sample Budget Report

10/08/91
1-1197

Budget vs Actual-Summary
For the Period 09/01/90 Through 09/30/91

Account Description	Current Period			Year-To-Date			Annual Budget
	Actual	Budget	Variance	Actual	Budget	Variance	
INCOME							
Assessment Current Year	78,007	78,549	-542	711,445	706,939	4,505	942,586
Assessment Prior Year	0	0	0	17,553	0	17,553	0
Carryover-Prior Year	0	0	0	0	0	0	0
Endowment Income	0	8,239	-8,239	48,775	74,153	-25,373	98,870
Endowment Inc-Restricted	0	6,809	-6,809	75,618	61,280	14,339	81,706
▓▓▓▓ Income	15	0	15	1,077	0	1,077	0
Gifts & Other Income	0	1,072	-1,072	15,193	9,647	5,546	12,863
Interest Income	466	250	216	4,958	2,250	2,708	3,000
Trustees Share of Expenses	0	0	0	7,500	7,500	0	10,000
DDF Share of Expenses	0	0	0	3,750	3,750	0	5,000
ADIF Share of Expenses	0	0	0	2,250	2,250	0	3,000
Other Income-Restricted	1,583	2,233	-650	16,617	20,097	-3,480	26,796
Other Income-Unrestricted	4,375	1,917	2,458	14,042	17,250	-3,208	23,000
▓▓▓ Income	0	0	0	68,139	0	68,139	0
Life Ins Reimbursement	0	0	0	351	0	351	0
TOTAL INCOME	84,445	99,068	-14,623	987,272	985,116	82,156	1,206,821

OPERATING EXPENSES

MINISTRY I							
Ministry Grants & I.R.P.	8,885	5,187	-3,698	91,029	84,259	-6,770	112,345
░░░░░░░░	5,106	5,106	0	45,954	45,951	-3	61,268
Group Life Insurance	0	1,900	1,900	5,894	5,700	-194	7,600
Medical Insurance-Retired	0	15,844	15,844	36,311	47,530	11,219	63,374
Medical Ins. Retired Spouses	0	15,140	15,140	31,469	45,417	13,948	60,557
░░░░░░░░	1,667	0	-1,667	9,463	9,900	437	13,200
░░░░░░░░	2,785	3,272	486	30,567	29,447	-1,119	39,263
MINISTRY I TOTAL	18,444	46,449	28,005	250,687	268,204	17,517	357,607
MINISTRY II							
░░░░░░░░	9,130	4,329	-4,800	100,117	38,963	-69,155	51,950
Christian Education-Director	0	0	0	341	3,750	3,409	5,000
Christian Education-Other	0	0	0	1,099	1,875	776	2,500
Evangelism & Renewal	125	150	25	1,819	1,350	-469	1,800
MINISTRY II TOTAL	9,254	4,479	-4,775	111,377	45,938	-65,440	61,250
MINISTRY III							
Hospital Chaplain	2,838	3,955	1,117	34,712	35,597	885	47,463
Counseling	3,000	3,000	0	27,000	27,000	0	36,000
University Ministry	0	0	0	0	0	0	0
MINISTRY III TOTAL	5,838	6,955	1,117	61,712	62,597	885	83,463
MINISTRY IV							
Clergy Spouse Conference	0	0	0	1,990	3,490	1,500	3,490
Commission on Ministry	78	385	307	1,170	3,461	2,291	4,615

www.ingramcontent.com/pod-product-compliance
Lightning Source LLC
Chambersburg PA
CBHW061841220326
41599CB00027B/5362